Talking About

Eating
Problems

Nicola Edwards

Chrysalis Children's Books

First published in the UK in 2003 by
Chrysalis Children's Books
An imprint of Chrysalis Books Group Plc
The Chrysalis Building
Bramley Road
London W10 6SP

Paperback edition first published in 2005

ISBN 184138 828 9 (hb)
ISBN 184458 317 1 (pb)

British Library Cataloguing in Publication Data for this book is available from the British Library.

Editorial manager: Joyce Bentley
Senior editor: Sarah Nunn
Picture researchers: Terry Forshaw, Lois Charlton
Designer: Wladek Szechter
Editor: Kate Phelps
Consultant: Dr Ute Navidi, Head of Policy, ChildLine

Printed in China

The pictures used in this book do not show the actual people named in the the text.

Foreword

News headlines screaming 'obscene' over two photos – one child starving, the other tucking into an oversize hamburger. In the global context it seems absurd that children in more affluent societies have eating problems. Yet food is a battleground or concern in many families.

Children pick up cues about body image from everywhere around them – from mums, older sisters, friends, media, fashion and pop idols. Non-judgemental and sensitive, **Talking About Eating Problems** explores why children can develop problems with food. It offers no quick fixes but helps adults unlock such children's often secretive world. To children struggling with worries about their weight or being bullied for having the 'wrong' shape, the book suggests alternative ways of dealing with the underlying problems. Without help, eating problems can get out of control, so identifying someone they can talk to – a trusted adult, a friend or ChildLine – means taking the first step towards settling into a healthier lifestyle.

Informative and thought-provoking, the **Talking About** series tackles some disturbing aspects of contemporary society: bullying, divorce, domestic violence, racism and eating problems. Adults often try to protect children from these problems or believe they will not understand. Taking children through a series of situations they can identify with – using words and images – also means offering alternative ways of resolving conflict. Each book shows that even very young children are not passive observers or victims but want to make sense of their world and act to make life better for themselves, their families and other children.

Ute Navidi, Head of Policy, ChildLine

contents

Problems with food

Many people go on **diets** and eat less to try to lose weight. Problems can start when people stop eating properly because they are so worried about putting on weight.

Wanting to be thin can make people very unhappy.

People can develop health problems if they eat too much and become **overweight**.

People can also have health problems if they eat more food than their bodies need and don't take enough **exercise**.

Eating too little or eating too much can damage people's health.

Who has eating problems?

Both girls and boys can have problems with overeating and not taking enough exercise.

Eating problems happen more in countries where there is plenty of food for everyone.

Problems with eating can happen to girls from rich and poor backgrounds, whose home lives may be very different.

Often it is teenage girls who are most at risk of developing problems by eating too little.
But teenage boys and younger children can also develop problems with food.

What is anorexia?

Anorexia nervosa is a type of eating problem. Someone who has anorexia deliberately avoids food or refuses to eat because they are afraid of putting on weight.

A person with anorexia may make excuses not to eat.

Starving the body of food is very dangerous.

People with anorexia may see themselves as fat, even while they are becoming thinner and thinner. They often wear baggy clothes to hide how thin they are.

What is bulimia?

Bulimia nervosa is an eating problem, which is similar to anorexia.

A person with bulimia may take food in secret, feeling guilty about what they are doing.

But rather than not eating, a person with bulimia will eat a large amount of food very quickly. Then they will make themselves sick or go to the toilet to get rid of the food. People with bulimia often feel very ashamed of what they do.

People with bulimia often have bodies that don't look **underweight**. This can make it harder for others to spot that they have an eating problem.

Eating too much

Some people use food to **comfort** themselves when they're feeling unhappy or bored. Comfort foods such as biscuits and chocolate bars often contain a lot of sugar and fat.

When there are lots of tempting snacks around, it is easy to eat more food than the body needs.

Eating a **balanced diet** with lots of fruit and vegetables is important for good health.

Eating too much sugar and fat can make people put on weight. Being overweight, or **obese**, can make people unhappy and lead to health problems.

Skinny people everywhere

Sometimes it seems that there are good-looking, skinny people everywhere. Most television presenters, film stars and pop idols are very slim. Even dolls have thin bodies with tiny waists.

Children often want to look like the people they see in magazines and on television.

This can make people think that they have to be thin to be popular and successful.

People's bodies are all sorts of shapes and sizes.

A child's body shape usually depends on what his or her parents look like.

Bullied for being fat or thin

Bullies often pick on people they see as being different in some way, especially in the way they look.

Johnny was bullied for being overweight. It made him feel very unhappy.

So children who are overweight or underweight are often an easy target for bullies. Being bullied can make children feel sad and **lonely**.

Children at school bullied Isabel because she found it hard to put on weight.

Be proud of yourself. Tell someone you **trust** if you are bullied.

Feelings about food

Children get ideas about food from television and magazines as well as from their friends.

People tend to eat more healthily if the family sits down to eat together.

Lucy's mum worried when Lucy said she would only eat foods that had no fat.

What happens at home affects them too. Parents may give young children sweets to **reward** them or comfort them when they are upset. Or if their mum is always on a diet, children may come to think that eating is wrong.

Feeling angry, feeling sad

Often, when people develop eating problems, it is a sign that they are unhappy.

Being told he was fat made Matt feel sad and alone. Then he ate more to try to cheer himself up.

Sometimes Anna felt left out at school. She thought she would be happier if she could be thinner.

Being overweight can make people feel **ashamed** and lose their **self-confidence**.

They may be angry or worried about something and use food to try to forget their problems. If someone is feeling helpless, they may starve themselves as a way of taking control of their bodies.

Worries and problems

Sometimes people's problems with eating are caused by difficulties at home or at school.

Lucy felt better
when she talked to her mum about
how she was feeling.

Some children feel they will never be good enough at school and that their bodies will never be thin enough. They put themselves under so much **pressure** that it makes them ill.

Toni felt under pressure to do as well as her sister at school.

If you are worried about something, tell someone you trust.

Getting help

If someone has an eating problem, it is very important that they talk about it. There are lots of people who can help.

People who are recovering from eating problems need to know they have support from their family and friends.

People with anorexia or
bulimia often go to hospital
to get better and meet with doctors
who can help them.

But the person with the problem often refuses to see that anything is wrong. That is very upsetting for the people who care about them.

If you know someone with an eating problem, encourage them to seek help for it.

Enjoyable eating

It is not helpful to think of good and bad foods. All foods are fine to eat if they are part of a balanced diet.

Our bodies need a range
of different foods.

Everyone can enjoy sugary, fatty foods as long as they don't eat too many of them.

Children need to eat well and drink plenty of water to grow and be healthy.

Eating food cannot make a sad person happy. Instead they need to talk about how they are feeling with someone they trust.

Look after yourself

As well as eating healthily, people need to look after their bodies by exercising regularly. It is good to spend some time every day in the fresh air, rather than sitting indoors in front of the TV or playing computer games.

True friends like each other for who they are – not for what they look like.

Enjoying
exercise helps you
feel good about yourself.
It can be a great way to
make friends, too.

Being fit and healthy helps people
to feel happy and confident.

Words to remember

ashamed Feeling bad, as if you have done something wrong.

balanced diet A mixture of different foods needed for good health, which may or may not include meat.

bullies People who hurt others or make them feel sad.

comfort Helping someone who is sad to feel better.

diet When someone eats only certain foods or limits the amount of food they eat to try to lose weight.

exercise Physical activity that helps keep a person healthy and fit.

lonely Feeling sad, as if you have no friends.

obese Being very overweight.

overweight Weighing more than is healthy for a person's height.

pressure Feeling forced to do something.

reward Giving somebody something for being good or doing well.

self-confidence Feeling as if you can do anything.

trust Feeling that someone won't let you down.

underweight Weighing less than is healthy for a person's height.

Organisations, helplines and websites

FOR CHILDREN:

ChildLine
A charity offering information, help and advice to any child with worries or problems.
Address for adults:
45 Folgate Street
London E1 6GL
Address for children:
Freepost NATN1111
London E1 6BR
Free and confidential helpline for children and young people: 0800 1111
ChildLine Scotland bullying helpline: 0800 441111
www.childline.org.uk

British Nutrition Foundation
Offers information on nutritional wellbeing.
www.nutrition.org.uk

Eating Disorders Association
Offers information and support on all aspects of eating disorders.
1st Floor, Wensum House
103 Prince of Wales Road
Norwich
Norfolk NR1 1DW
Youth helpline (4pm to 6.30pm Monday to Friday):
0845 634 7650
www.edauk.com/young_home.htm

Central Council of Physical Recreation
An organisation that promotes sport at all levels.
www.ccpr.org.uk

Sport England
A body that aims to get more people involved in sport.
www.sportengland.org

FOR PARENTS:

National Centre for Eating Disorders
Offers treatment and support for those affected by eating disorders.
54 New Road
Esher
Surrey KT10 9NU
www.eating-disorders.org.uk

Association for the Study of Obesity
Provides information on the causes, prevention and treatment of obesity.
20 Brook Meadow Close
Woodford Green
Essex IG8 9NR
www.aso.org.uk

Index

Picture credits
Front cover (main) Bubbles/Pauline Cutler, front cover left to right: Getty Images/Donna Day, Bubbles/Loisjoy Thurstun, Bubbles/Ian West, Photofusion/Ute Klaphake, 4 Photofusion/Ute Klaphake, 5 Getty Images/Donna Day, 6 Bubbles/Pauline Cutler, 7 Bubbles/Angela Hampton, 8 Bubbles/Chris Rout, 9 Photofusion/Paul Baldesare, 10 Science Photo Library/Oscar Burriel, 11-12 Bubbles/Chris Rout, 13 Corbis/Michael Heron, 14 Corbis/Tom & Dee Ann McCarthy, 15 Corbis/Jennie Woodcock, 16 Getty Images/Photodisc, 17 Getty Images/Color Day, 18 Corbis/Ariel Skelley, 19 Bubbles/David Robinson, 20 Bubbles/Pauline Cutler, 21 Getty Images/Jim Whitmer, 22 Bubbles/David Robinson, 23 Getty Images/Ian Shaw, 24 Getty Images/Photo Disc, 25 Bubbles/Frans Rombout, 26-27 Bubbles/Loisjoy Thurstun, back cover Bubbles/Chris Rout